AMERICAN HEROES

ABRAHAM LINCOLN
A Courageous Leader

AMERICAN HEROES

ABRAHAM LINCOLN
A Courageous Leader

SNEED B. COLLARD III

mc **Marshall Cavendish**
Benchmark
New York

For Sammie Garnett,
dear friend, gifted teacher, and passionate patriot

Marshall Cavendish Benchmark
99 White Plains Road
Tarrytown, New York 10591-9001
www.marshallcavendish.us

Library of Congress Cataloging-in-Publication Data
Collard, Sneed B.
Abraham Lincoln: a courageous leader / by Sneed B. Collard III.
p. cm. — (American heroes)
Includes bibliographical references and index.
Summary: "A juvenile biography of Abraham Lincoln, our sixteenth president"—Provided by publisher.
ISBN-13: 978-0-7614-2162-7
ISBN-10: 0-7614-2162-9
1. Lincoln, Abraham, 1809–1865—Juvenile literature. 2. Presidents—United States—Biography—
Juvenile literature. I. Title. II. Series: Collard, Sneed B. American heroes.
E457.905.C63 2007
973.7092—dc22 [B]   2006013119

Editor: Joyce Stanton
Editorial Director: Michelle Bisson
Art Director: Anahid Hamparian
Series Designer and Compositor: Anne Scatto / PIXEL PRESS
Printed in Malaysia
1 3 5 6 4 2

Images provided by Rose Corbett Gordon, Art Editor,
Mystic, CT, from the following sources:
Front cover: Getty Images
Back cover: North Wind Picture Archives
Page i, 34: Getty Images; *pages ii, 23:* The Art Archive/
Culver Pictures; *pages vi, 19, 24, 27:* Super Stock;
pages 1, 12, 15, 20, 28, 31: The Granger Collection, NY;
Page 3: Artwork by Lloyd Ostendorf, Courtesy
of the Ostendorf family; *pages 4, 8:* Hulton rchive/Getty
Images; *page 7:* Bettmann/Corbis; *page 11:* Chicago
Historical Society/ Bridgeman Art Library;
page 16: Private Collection/ Bridgeman Art Library;
page 32: North Wind Picture Archives

CONTENTS

Abraham Lincoln always worked hard.
Here, he helps his father build a new family home.

Abraham Lincoln

As a boy, Abraham Lincoln learned that life was hard. Very hard. One day when he was three or four years old, Abraham helped his father plant pumpkin seeds. A few days later, a flash flood washed away the entire field. When he was nine years old, Abraham's mother became sick and died. Her death made life even harder for the Lincoln family. But Abraham learned an important lesson. If life beat you down, you had to rise back up again.

Abraham Lincoln was the sixteenth president of the United States. In many ways, he was the most unlikely. He was born in 1809 in a log cabin in Kentucky. His parents worked hard, but were poor. His father, Thomas, struggled as a carpenter and a farmer. His mother, Nancy, could not read or write, but she told Abraham and his older sister, Sarah, Bible stories every night.

Nancy Lincoln could not read or write, but she told her children Bible stories every night.

Abraham was well known for his skill at using an axe.

Abraham grew into a tall, spindly youth. He wore clothes made from buckskin. He grew strong clearing fields and harvesting wheat. He was so good with an axe that one man said, "You would say there was three men at work by the way the trees fell."

As a boy, Abraham loved listening to his father swap stories with other men. Soon, Abraham became a storyteller himself. He especially loved funny stories. His sense of humor helped him survive the hardships he faced—and would face in the future.

Abraham had little time for school. But now and then, he did get to take a few classes. He learned to write. He also fell in love with reading. Soon, he carried a book everywhere he went. He even read while plowing fields. While the horse rested between rows, Abraham read a page or two. Then he plowed the next row. Books showed Lincoln that there was more to life than hard work, illness, and death.

Books showed Lincoln that there was
more to life than hard work and suffering.

In Illinois, Abraham earned money by working at Denton Offutt's General Store.

In 1830, the Lincoln family moved to Illinois. Here, Abraham determined to make a better life for himself. In the town of New Salem, he got a job in a general store. He joined a local debating group. He began giving speeches in his high, shrill voice. More than anything, he studied politics and the law.

Abraham Lincoln loved government. In 1832, at the age of twenty-three, he decided to run for the state assembly. He lost the election. But two years later, he ran again. This time he won. As an elected public official, Lincoln voted to build railroads and canals that would help the people of Illinois. He also taught himself the law and became a lawyer.

*Lincoln lost his first election, but two years later he was
elected to the Illinois State Assembly.*

Lincoln enjoyed the time he could spend with his family.

In 1837 Lincoln moved to Springfield, the new Illinois state capital. He built up a thriving law practice. Five years later, he married Mary Todd. Abraham and Mary had four sons. Abraham enjoyed wrestling with his sons and talking to Mary, but he never quit thinking about politics.

The most important issue of the day was slavery

Americans had owned slaves for two hundred years. Originally, most slaves came from Africa. They were kidnapped and sent to America. Slaves were forced to work long hours. They were whipped, beaten, and killed. Their children were also slaves. At any moment, a slave owner could sell children, wives, or husbands to another slave owner, and families would be separated forever.

*In Lincoln's time, many Americans owned slaves. Slaves had no say
at all about what happened to them or their families.*

Many Northerners wanted to stamp out slavery. Most Southerners wanted slavery to continue.

In Northern states, slavery was no longer legal. But in Southern states, slavery was widespread. In 1850, more than *three million* men, women, and children lived as slaves. Many Northerners wanted to stamp out slavery completely. Most Southerners wanted slavery to continue. As a boy, Abraham had seen slaves chained together. He watched how they were treated like animals.

As an adult, Lincoln hated slavery. He joined a new political party. It was created to stop the spread of slavery. It was called the Republican Party. In 1860 the Republican Party chose Lincoln to run for president of the United States.

Lincoln won.

In 1860 Lincoln was elected president of the United States.

The Civil War was a terrible conflict between Northerners and Southerners.
In the beginning, the Confederate army won many battles.

Southerners feared that President Lincoln would try to free the slaves. Lincoln did not think he could do that by law. Southerners did not believe him. After Lincoln became president, eleven Southern states voted to secede from, or leave, the United States. In 1861, to keep the country together, Lincoln went to war.

Most Northerners thought the Civil War would be over in a few months. They were wrong. Under General Robert E. Lee, the Southern, or "Confederate," army won battle after battle.

Lincoln learned fast, however. He taught himself about war and leading a nation. He found honest men to provide his Northern, or "Union," army with guns and supplies.

Still, life was not easy for Lincoln. He felt deep pain over the men killed in battle. And in February 1862, his eleven-year-old son Willie died of a fever. Willie's death crushed the Lincolns. Abraham sank into depression. His wife, Mary, suffered a nervous breakdown.

The death of young Willie crushed Abraham and Mary.

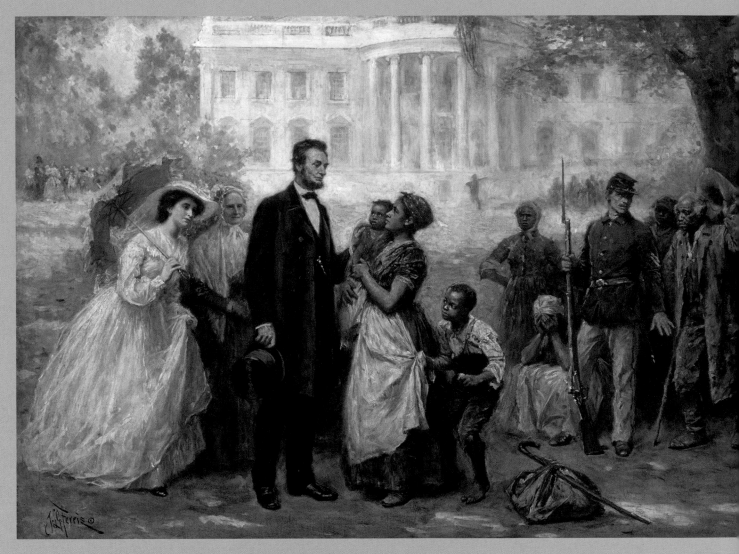

In 1863 Lincoln announced that all slaves
in Southern states were free.

But as he always had, Lincoln picked himself up again. On January 1, 1863, he issued the Emancipation Proclamation. In it, he declared that all slaves in the South were free "thenceforward and forever." Now the war wasn't just about keeping the nation together. It was about freeing the slaves, too.

There was just one problem. The slaves couldn't be free until the North won the war.

In 1863 the Union army defeated the Confederates near the town of Gettysburg, Pennsylvania. The following spring, Lincoln found a strong general, Ulysses S. Grant, to lead the Union soldiers. These two events helped turn the tide of the war. In November 1864, Lincoln was re-elected president. Finally, in April 1865, the Confederate army surrendered to Union forces.

The Civil War was over.

Lincoln gave a famous speech after the battle of Gettysburg,
one that our nation will long remember.

Lincoln grieved for the many men who lost their lives
fighting in the Civil War.

Lincoln was overjoyed that the war had ended. Now, the nation could begin to heal. But the war years had taken a terrible toll on him. Pain showed in every deep wrinkle of Lincoln's face.

He had lost his son Willie. His wife Mary's mind had "gone to pieces." And he lived knowing that he had sent hundreds of thousands of men to die in battle.

The end of the war was not the end of his suffering. On April 14, 1865, President Lincoln was watching a play with Mary. An angry Southerner, John Wilkes Booth, crept up behind them. He shot the president in the head. Lincoln died early the next morning, at 7:22 A.M. One of his closest friends, Secretary of War Edwin Stanton, said, "Now he belongs to the ages."

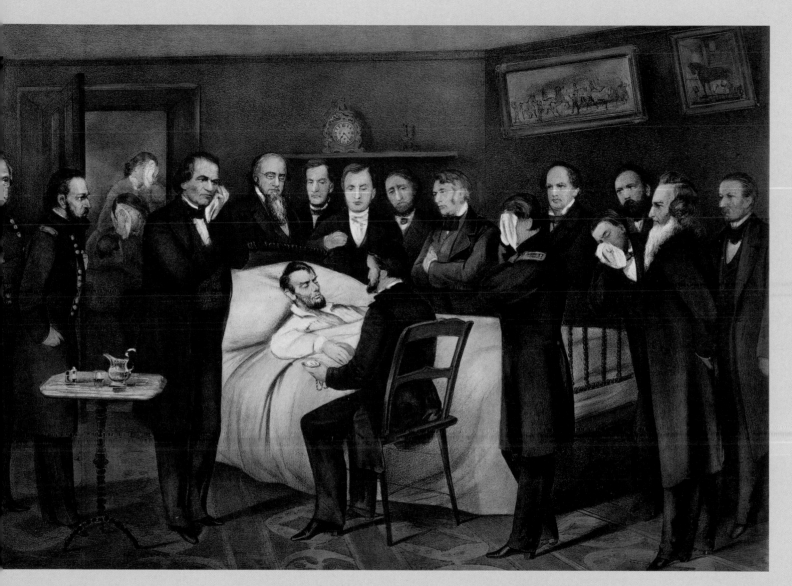

*Lincoln died at 7:22 A.M., April 15, 1865,
less than a week after the Civil War ended.*

*For his leadership and courage, Lincoln will always be
remembered as one of our greatest presidents.*

Today, more than 140 years after his death, we still remember Abraham Lincoln. During our country's worst times, he held our nation together. He freed millions of slaves. He planned for a future when all people would have the chance to improve their lives. For as long as our nation exists, Lincoln will remind us of who we are—and, if we work hard, what we can become.

Important Dates

1809 Born February 12 on Nolin Creek, Kentucky, to Thomas and Nancy Lincoln.

1816 Thomas Lincoln moves the family to Indiana.

1818 Nancy Lincoln dies.

1819 Thomas Lincoln marries Sarah Bush Johnston.

1830 Lincoln family moves to Illinois.

1832 Abraham Lincoln runs for first political office and loses.

1834 Wins first election, a seat in the state legislature of Illinois.

1836 Passes law exam to become a lawyer.

1842 Marries Mary Ann Todd.

1860 Elected president of the United States.

1861 The Civil War begins.

1862 Young Willie Lincoln dies.

1863 President Lincoln issues the Emancipation Proclamation, freeing all slaves in the Southern states.

1863 The Confederate army is defeated at Gettysburg.

1864 Lincoln is re-elected president of the United States.

1865 General Robert E. Lee surrenders the main Confederate army to Union forces on April 9; the Civil War ends.

1865 President Lincoln is shot by John Wilkes Booth; he dies the morning of April 15 at 7:22 A.M.

WORDS TO KNOW

buckskin A soft, strong leather made from the skins of deer or sheep.

Civil War The great war from 1861–1865 between the North and the South.

Confederate A person who supported the South during the Civil War.

debate To argue for or against something.

harvesting Gathering crops.

legal Allowed by law.

political party A group of voters who share a common set of values and beliefs.

politics The work or study of government.

slave A person who is owned by another person.

state assembly A branch of government that makes laws for a state.

Union The North during the Civil War, which supported the nation staying together.

TO LEARN MORE ABOUT ABRAHAM LINCOLN

WEB SITES

Abraham Lincoln Online.org
　　http://showcase.netins.net/web/creative/lincoln.html
Abraham Lincoln Research Site
　　http://members.aol.com/RVSNorton/Lincoln2.html
White House Site
　　www.whitehouse.gov/history/presidents/al16.html

BOOKS

Abe Lincoln Goes to Washington, 1837–1865 by Cheryl Harness.
　　National Geographic Society, 1997.

Abe Lincoln Remembers by Ann Turner. HarperCollins, 2000.

A Picture Book of Abraham Lincoln by David A. Adler. Holiday
　　House, 1989.

Young Abe Lincoln: The Frontier Days, 1809–1837 by Cheryl
　　Harness. National Geographic Society, 2003.

For more detailed photographs of President Lincoln, see also:

Lincoln: A Photobiography by Russell Freedman. Clarion Books, 1987.

Picturing Lincoln: Famous Photographs that Popularized the President by George Sullivan. Clarion Books, 2000.

PLACES TO VISIT

Gettysburg National Military Park
97 Taneytown Road, Gettysburg, Pennsylvania 17325
PHONE: (717) 334-1124   WEB SITE: **www.nps.gov/gett**

Lincoln Home National Historic Site
413 South Eighth Street, Springfield, Illinois 62701
PHONE: (217) 492-4241 ext 221   WEB SITE: **www.nps.gov/liho**

The Lincoln Memorial
23rd Street, NW, Washington, DC
PHONE: (202) 426-6841   WEB SITE: **www.nps.gov/linc/home.htm**

Lincoln's New Salem State Historic Site
15588 History Lane, Petersburg, Illinois 62675
PHONE: (217) 632-4000   WEB SITE: **www.lincolnsnewsalem.com**

INDEX

Page numbers for illustrations are in boldface.

ABOUT THE AUTHOR

SNEED B. COLLARD III is the author of more than fifty award-winning books for young people, including *The Prairie Builders; A Platypus, Probably; One Night in the Coral Sea*; and the four-book SCIENCE ADVENTURES series for Marshall Cavendish Benchmark. In addition to his writing, Sneed is a popular speaker and presents widely to students, teachers, and the general public. In 2006, he was selected as the Washington Post–Children's Book Guild Nonfiction Award winner for his achievements in children's writing. He is also the author of several novels for young adults, including *Dog Sense* and *Flash Point*. To learn more about Sneed, investigate his Web site at www.sneedbcollardiii.com.